The 'Mary Had a Little Lamb' Book

for Viola

by Cassia Harvey

CHP170

www.charveypublications.com - print books & free sheet music blog
www.learnstrings.com - PDF downloadable books & chamber music

1. Mary Had a Little Lamb

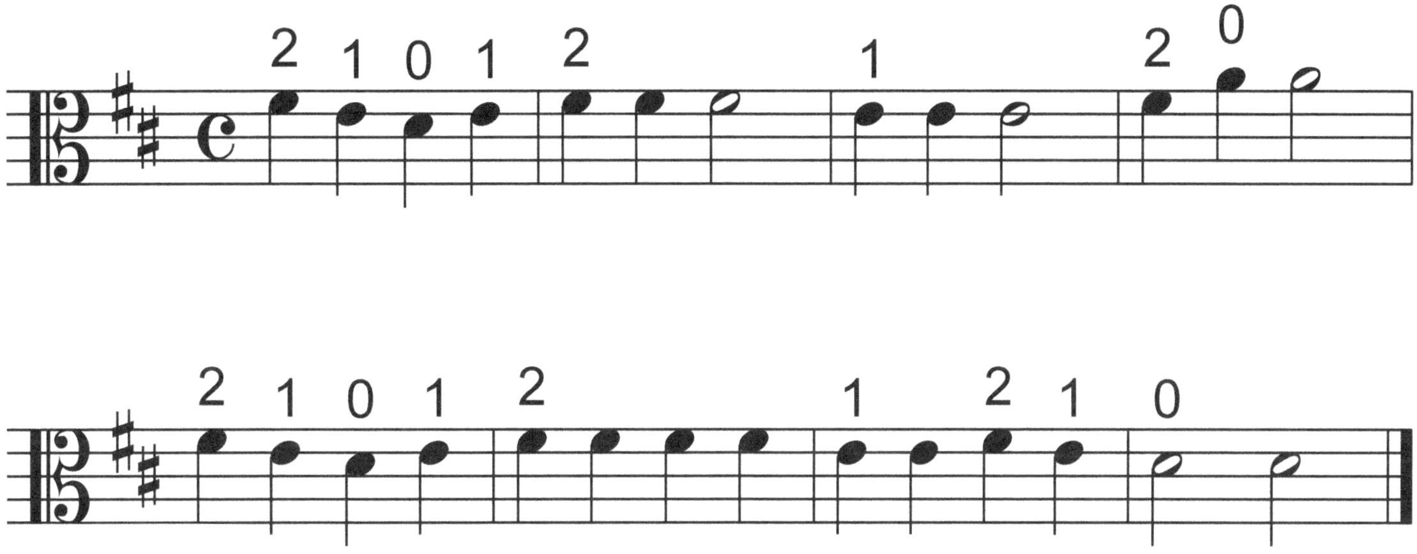

2. Mary Had Some Whole Notes

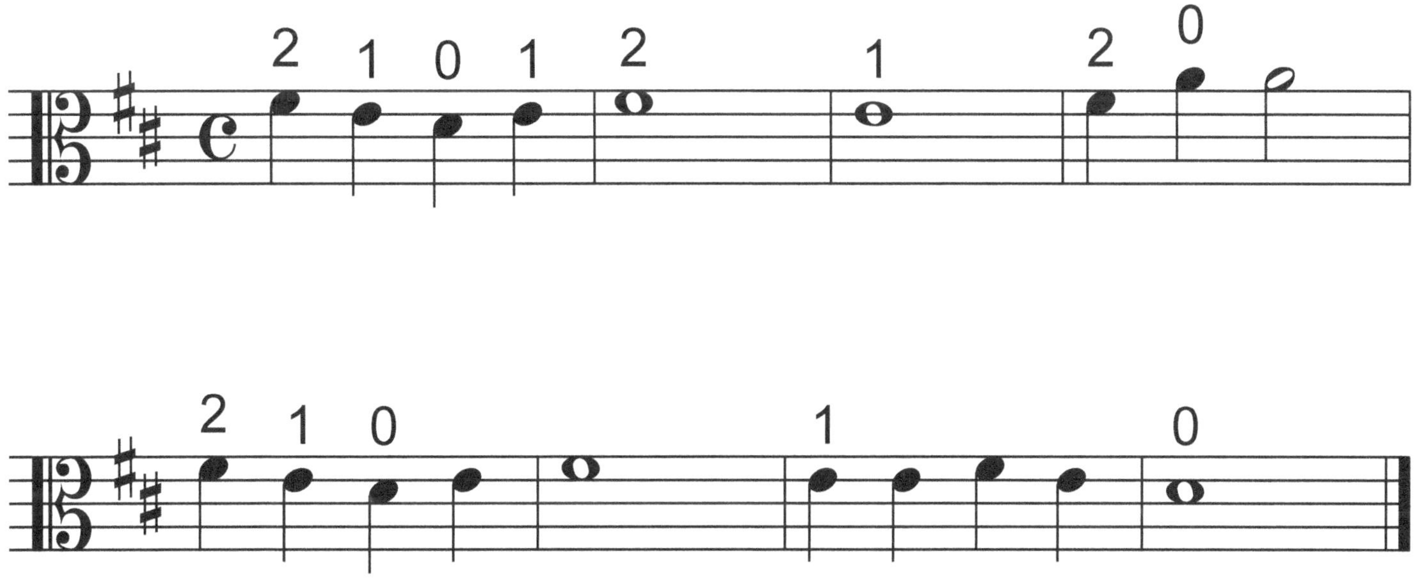

3. Mary Runs After the Lamb

4. Mary's Rhythm

5. Running and Crossing Strings

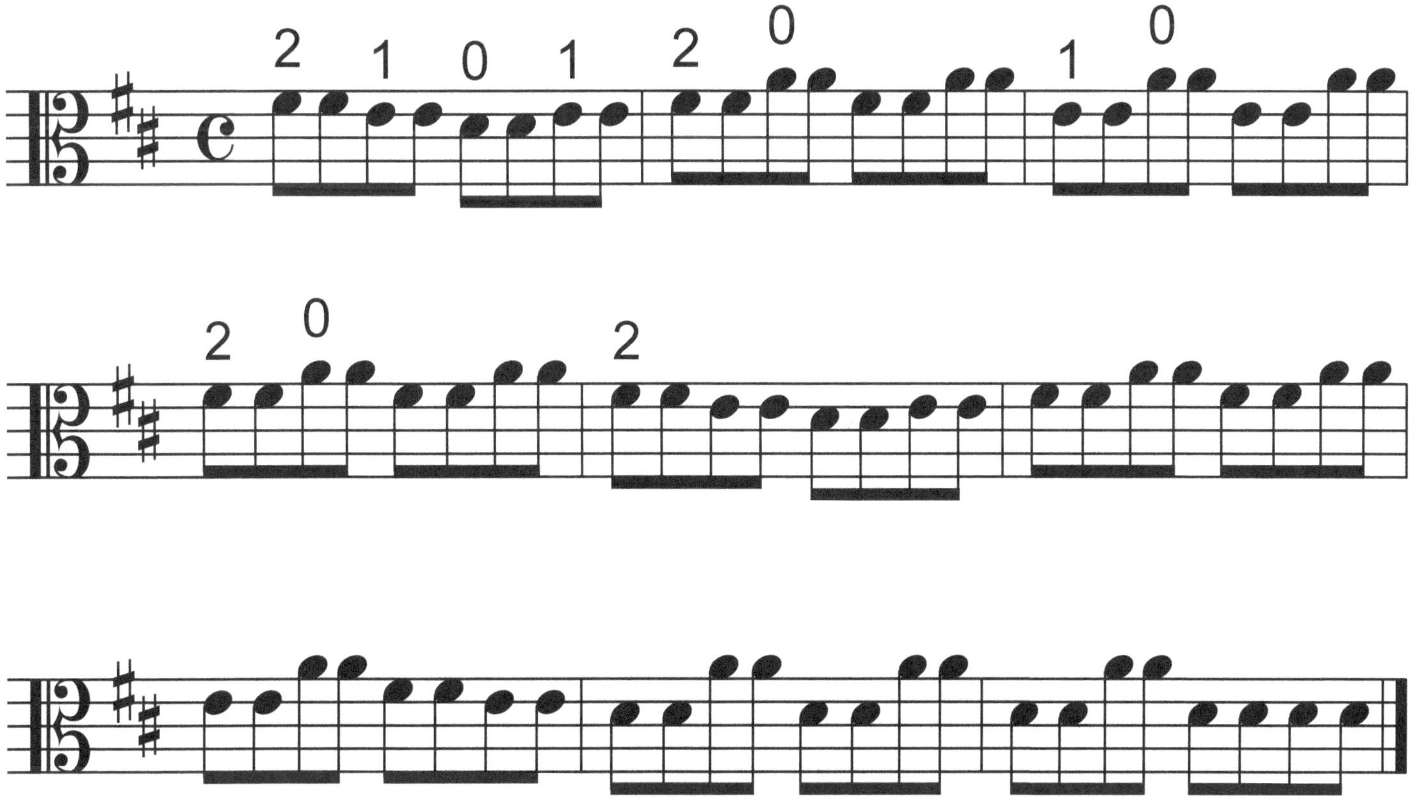

6. Mary Had a Little Lamb on A

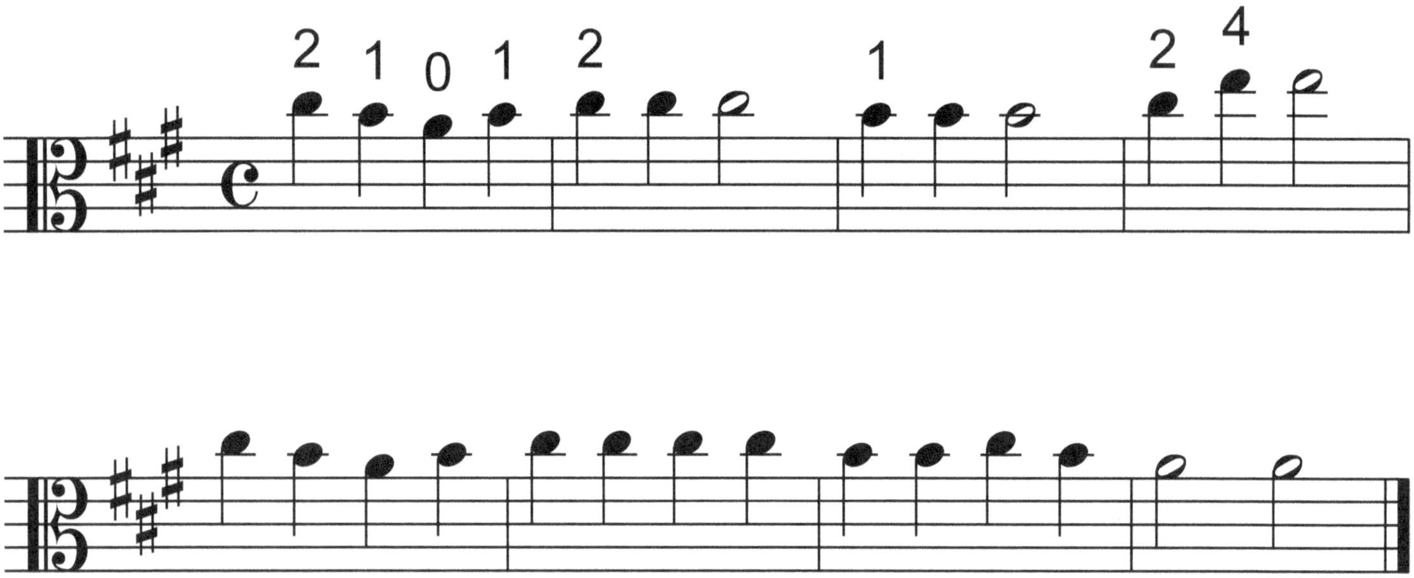

7. Lamb's Rhythm

8. Mary is Marching

9. Playing Slurs with Mary

10. Mary Had a Little Lamb on G

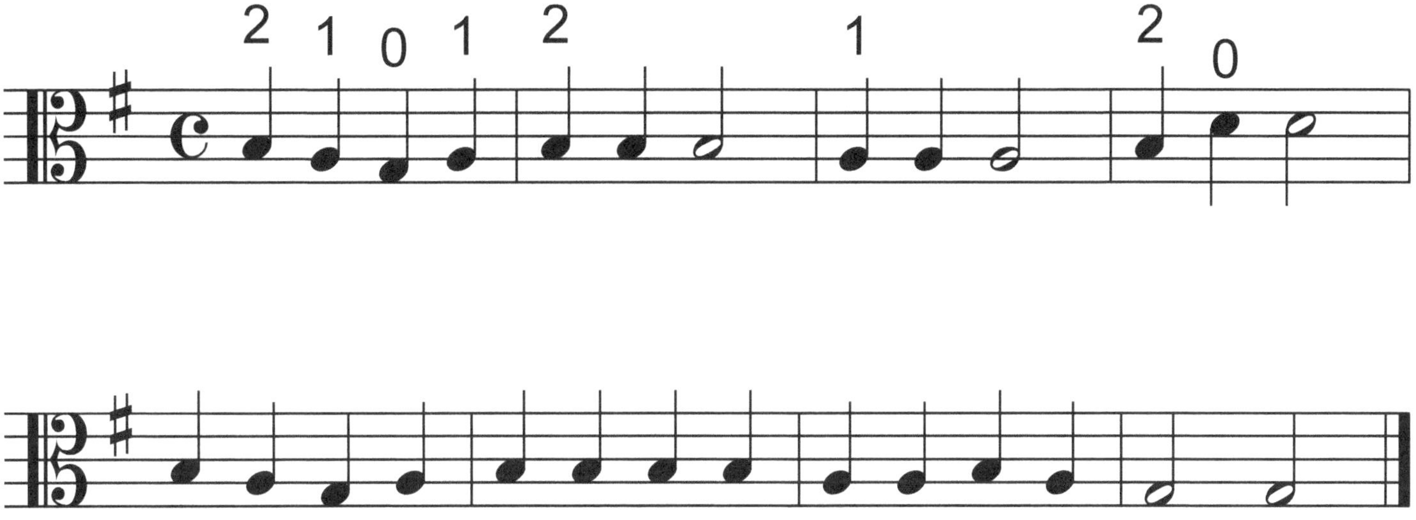

11. Lamb Rhythm

12. Mary's String Changing

13. Mary's Finger Exercise

14. Mary Had a Little Lamb on C

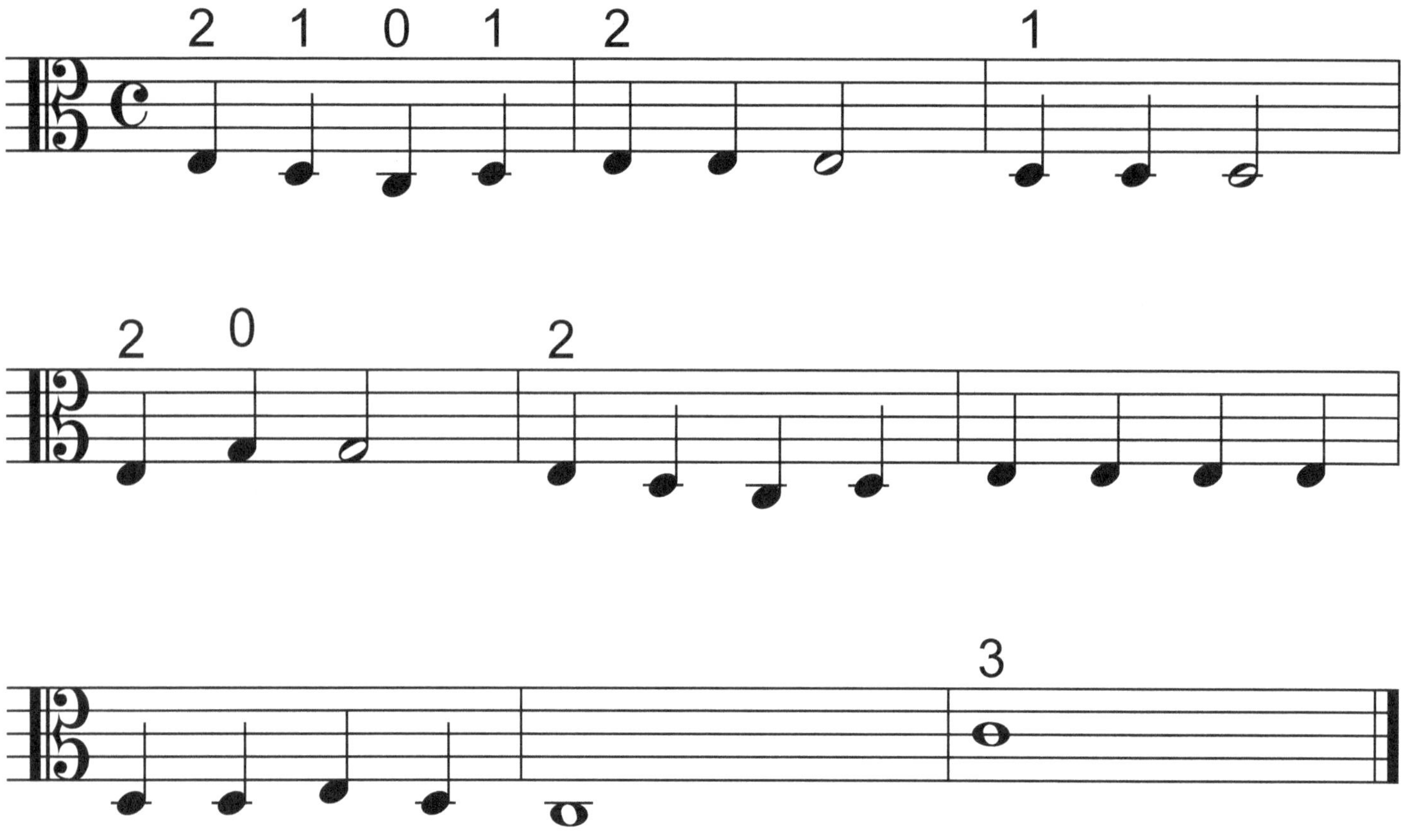

15. Lamb With Dotted Half Notes

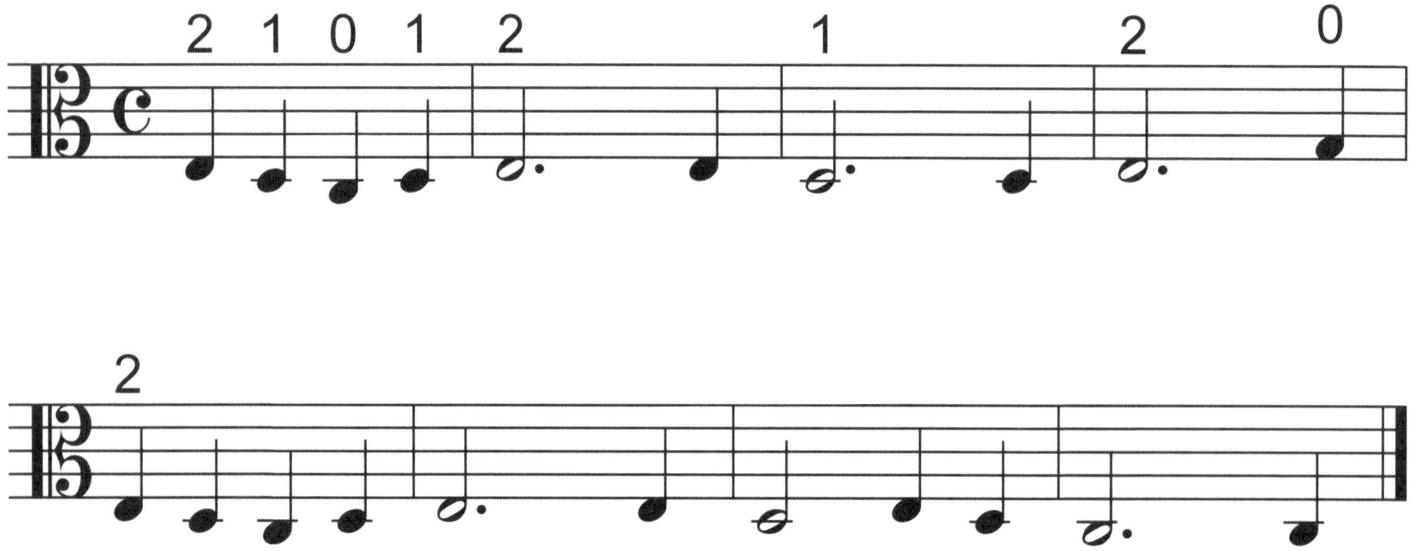

16. Mary's Rhythm

17. Mary Changes Strings

18. Mary Lost Her Little Lamb

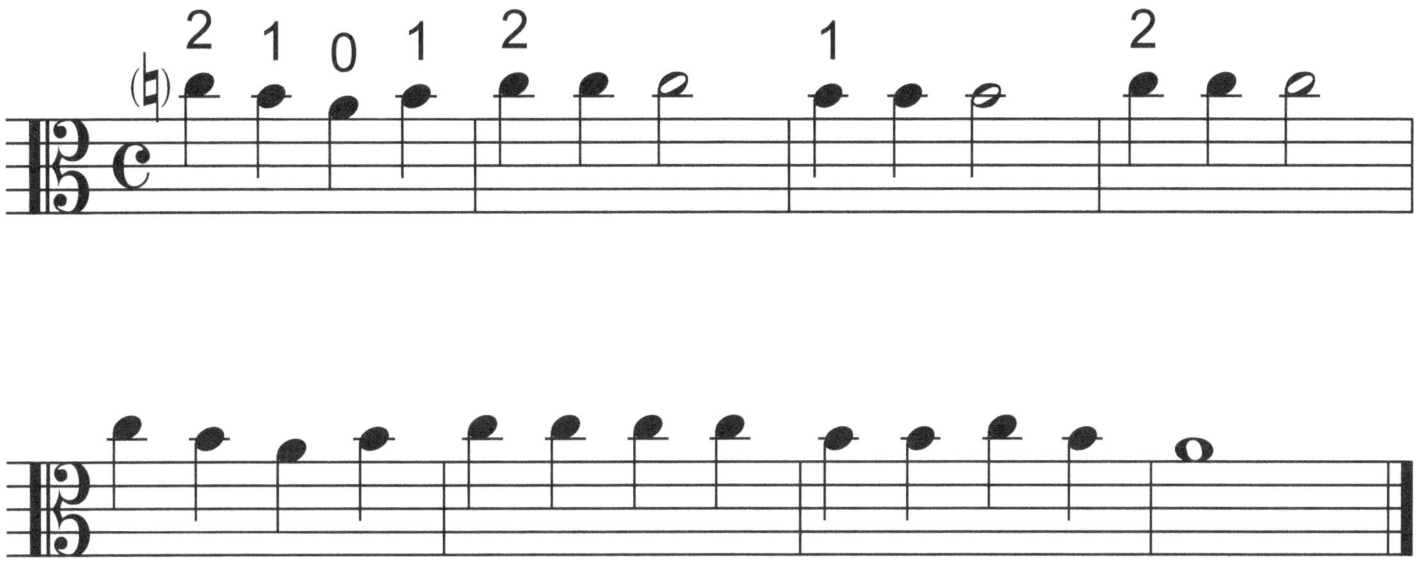

19. Lost Lamb Slurs

20. Mary Lost Her Little Lamb on D

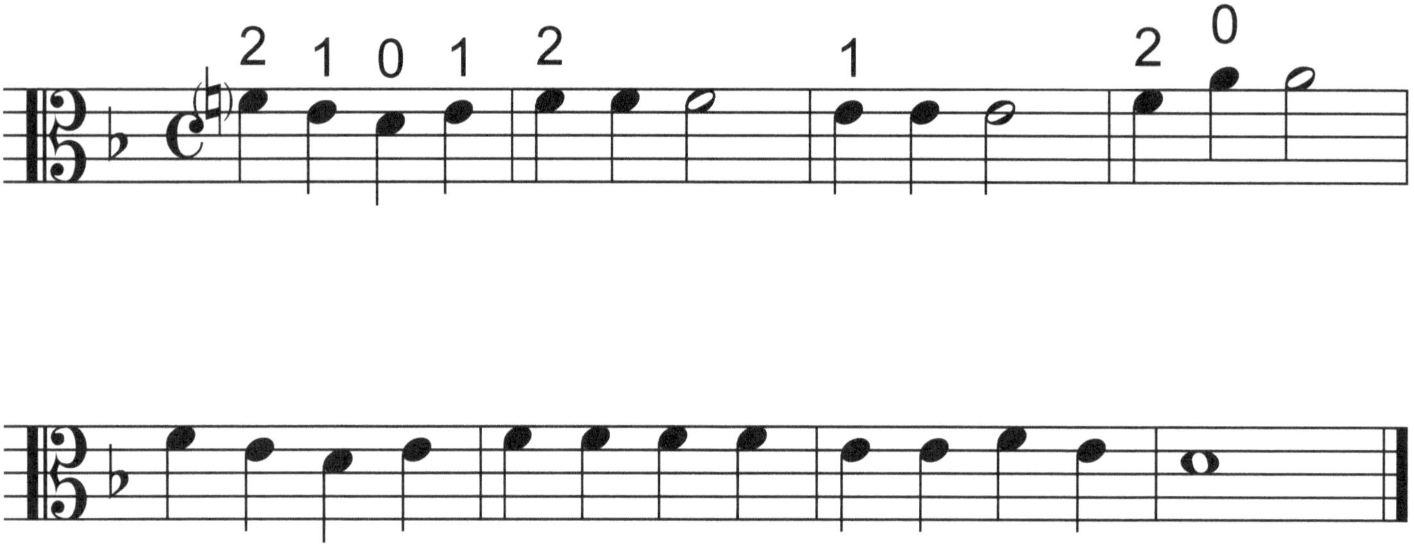

21. Lost Lamb in 3/4

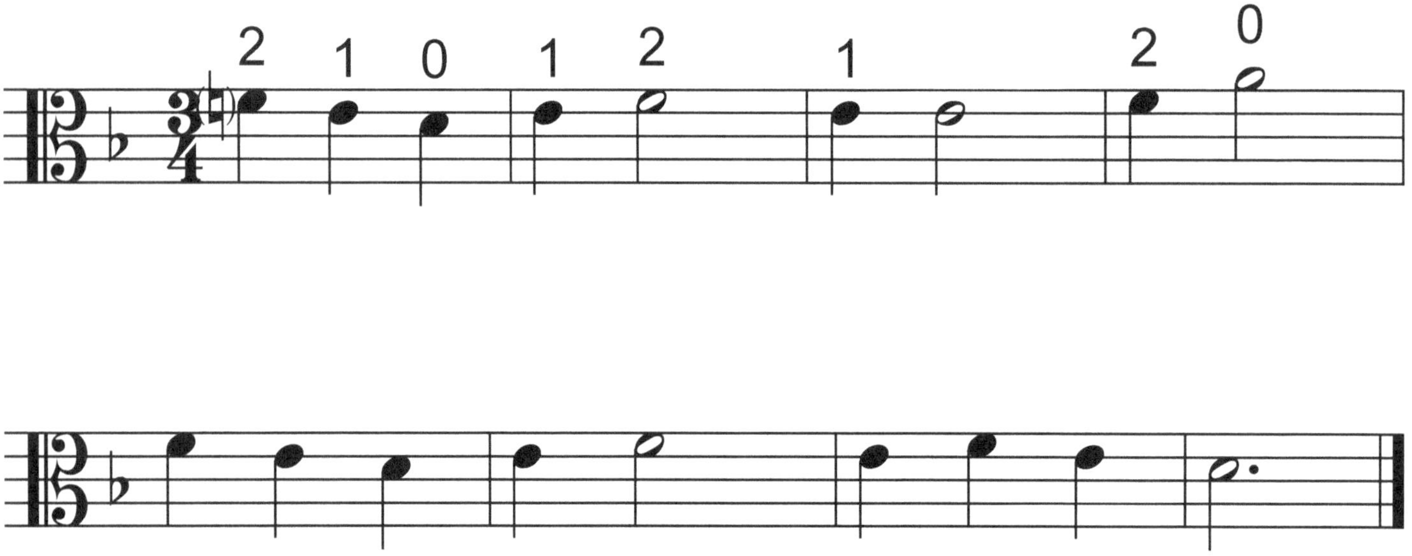

22. Mary Lost Her Little Lamb on G

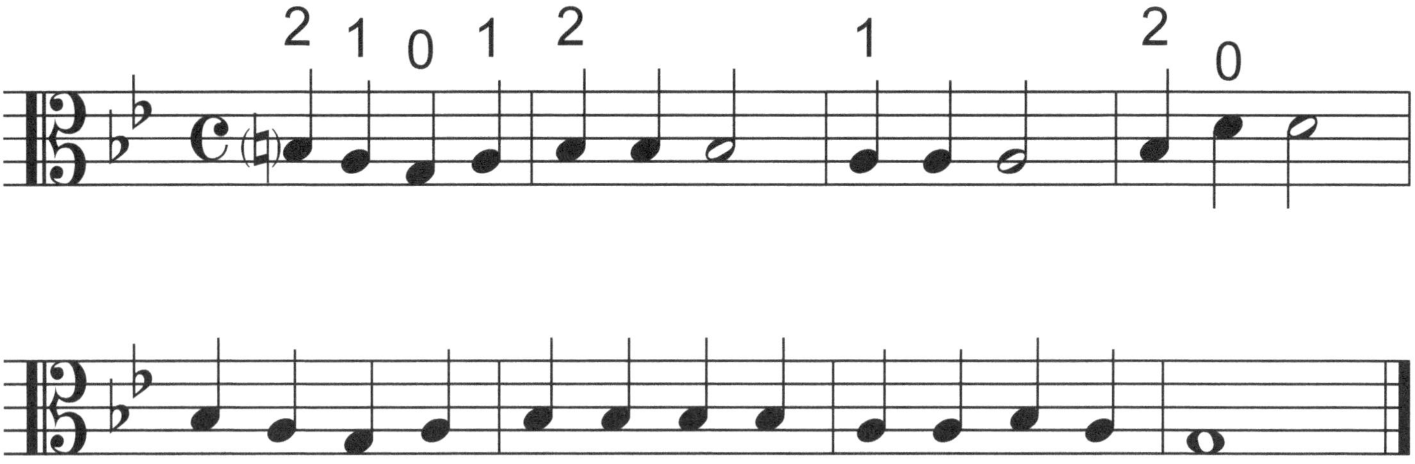

23. Lost Lamb in 6/8

24. Mary Lost Her Little Lamb on C

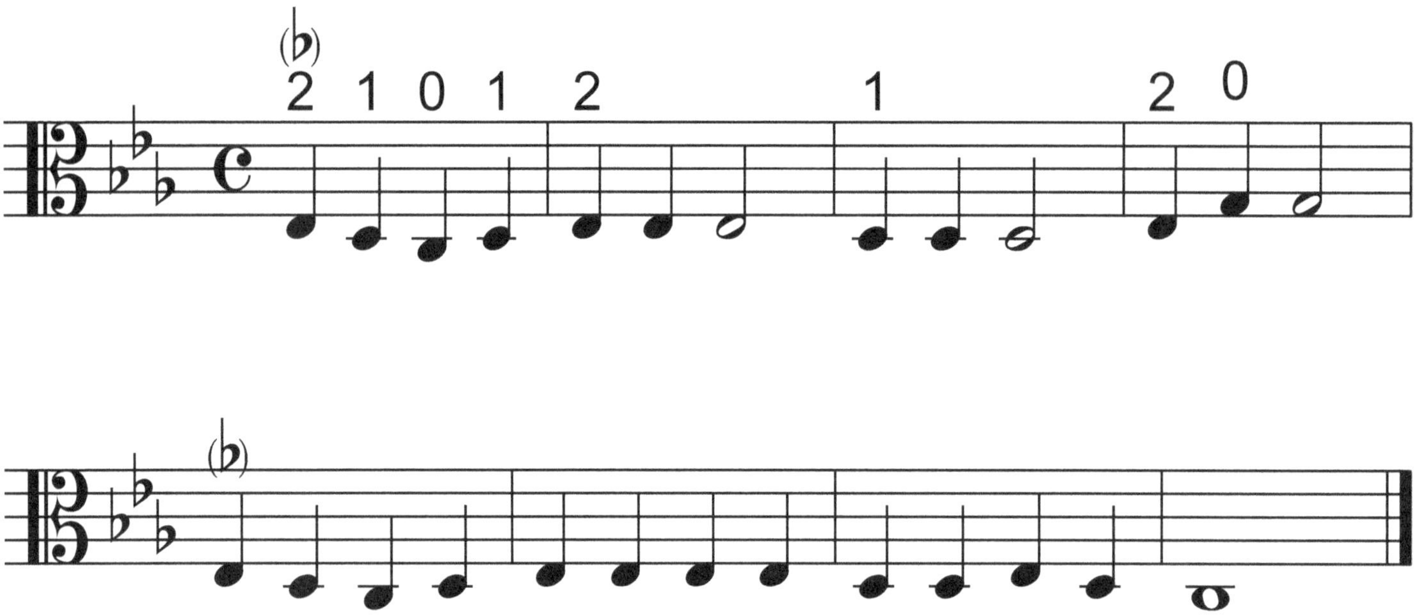

25. Lost Lamb in 2/4

26. Mary Starts on First Finger

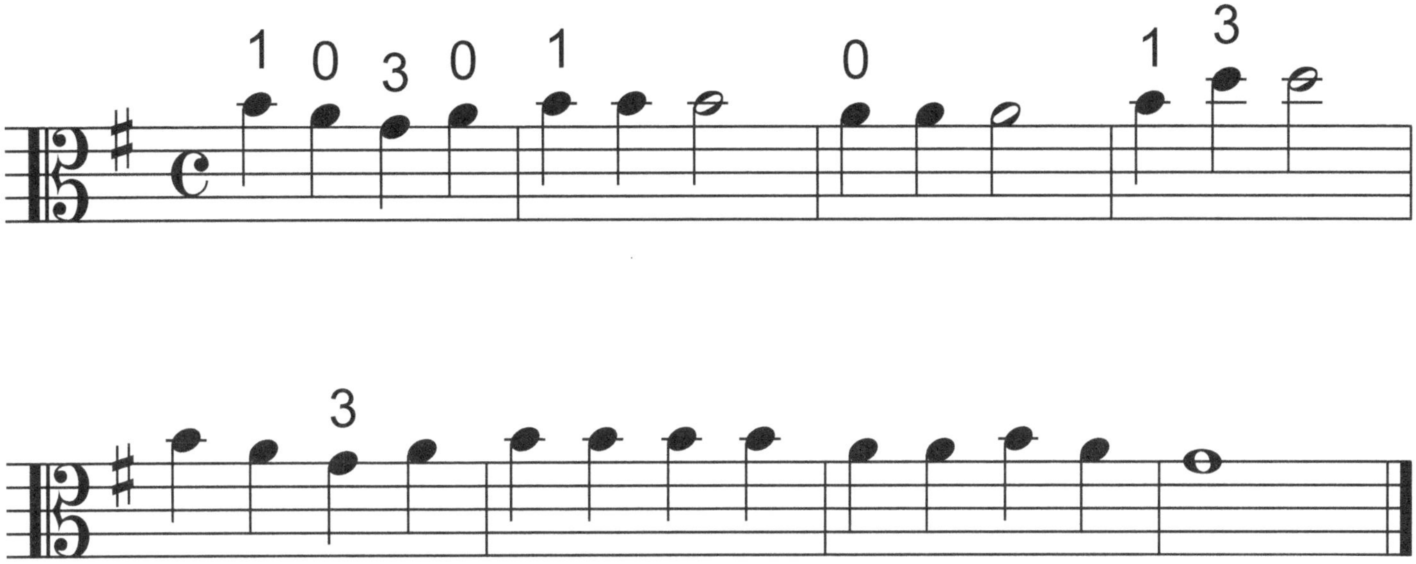

27. Lamb Slurs

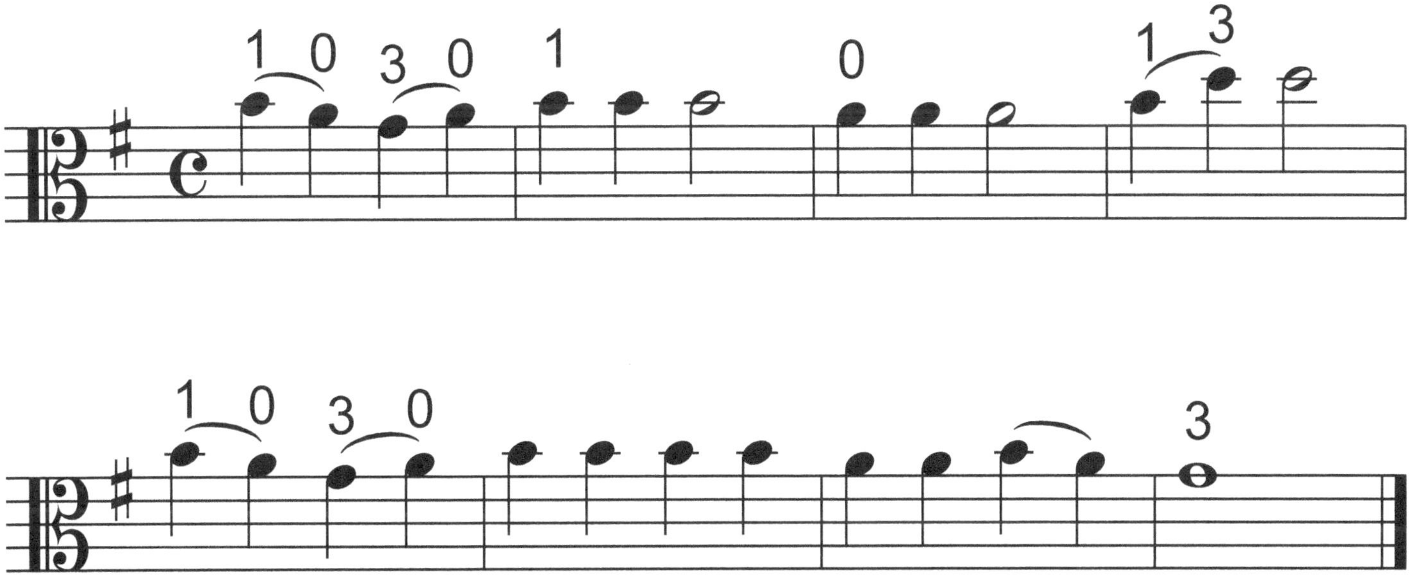

28. Mary's 6/8 Counting

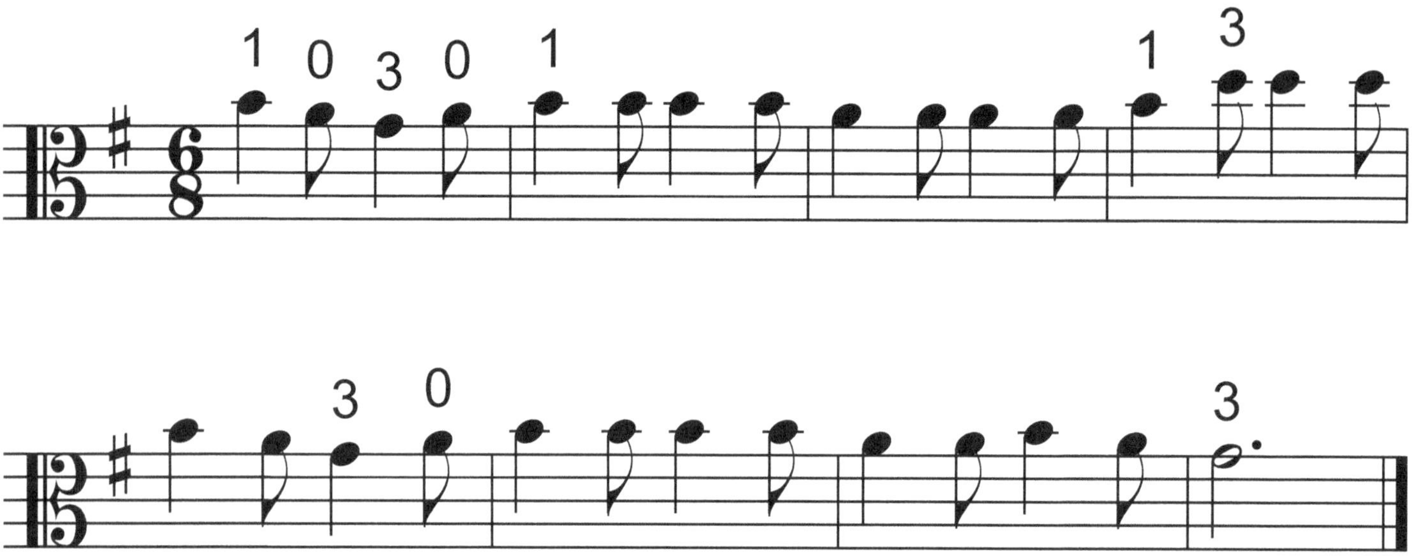

29. Lamb Stops

30. Mary Starts on First Finger

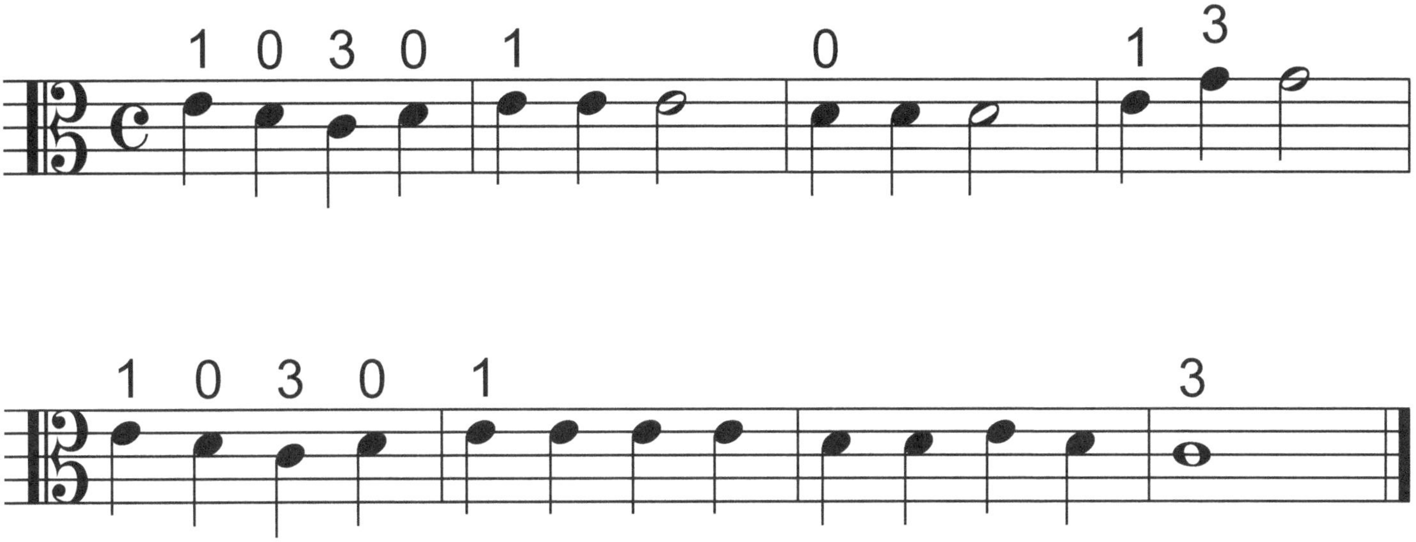

31. Mary's Rhythm

32. Lamb Slurs

33. Mary Starts on First Finger

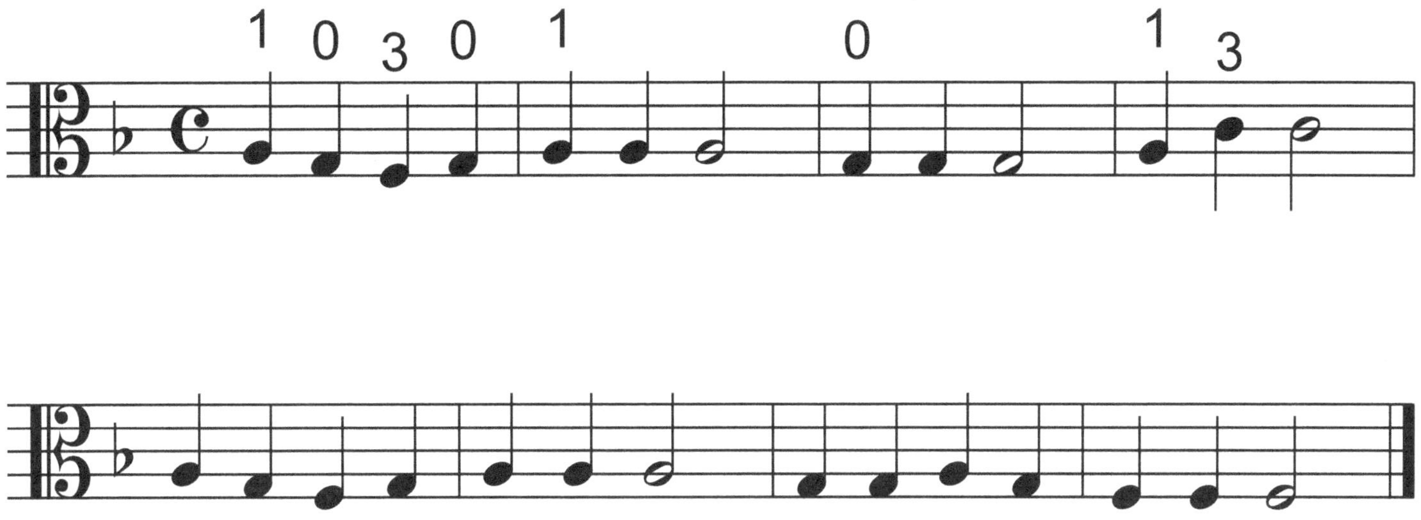

34. Lamb Dance in 6/8

35. Mary's Slurs

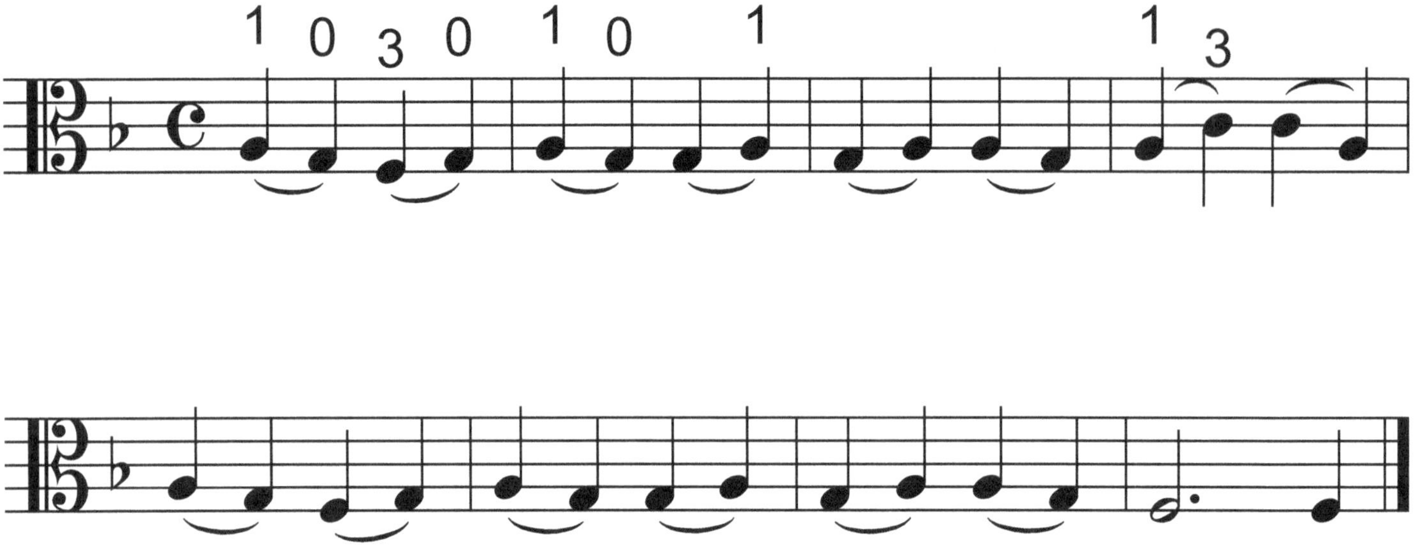

36. Mary Goes Running

37. Mary Starts on Open A

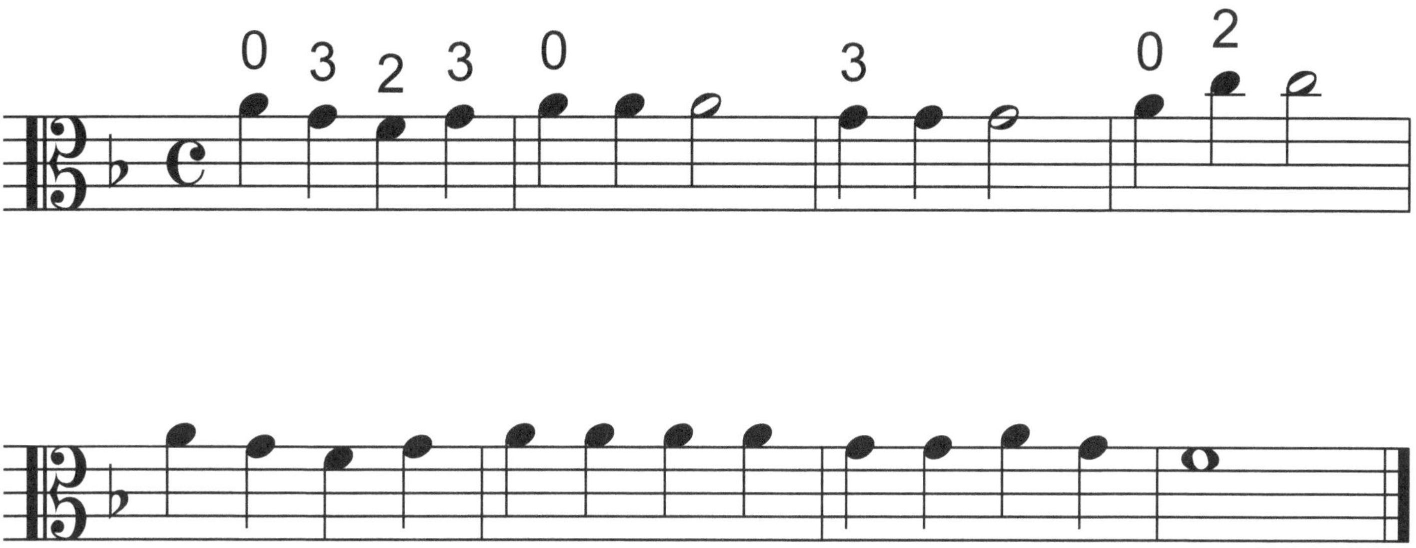

38. Lamb Crossing

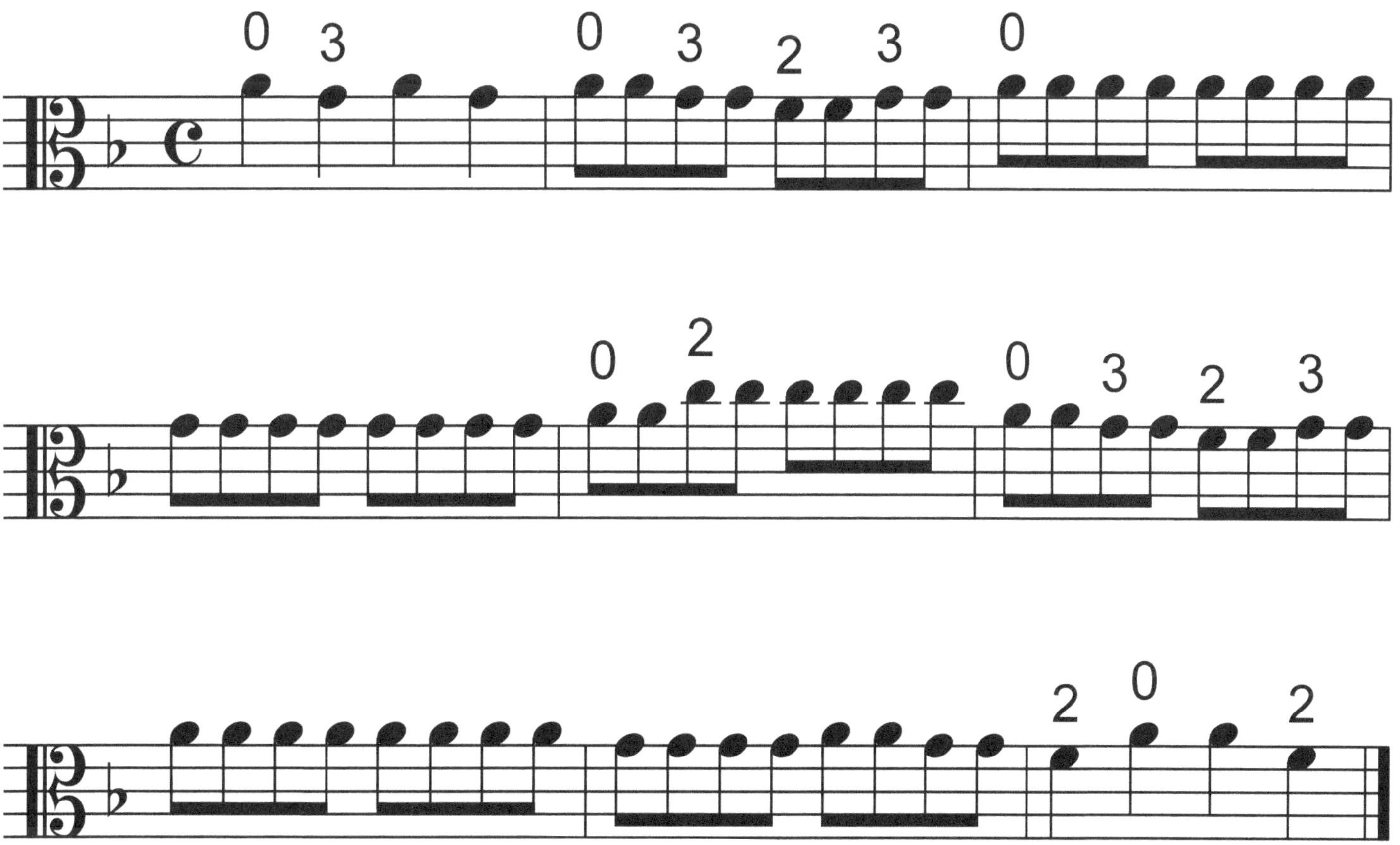

39. Mary's Rhythm

40. Mary Starts on Open D

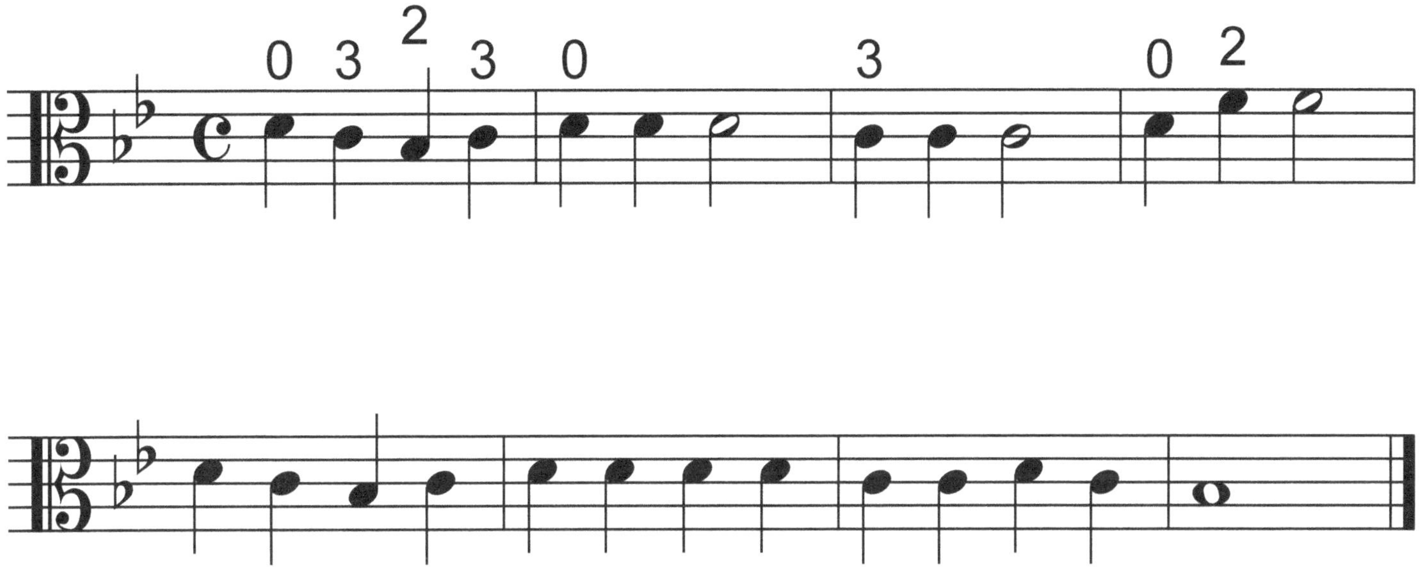

41. Mary's Dotted Quarter Notes

42. Mary in 3/4

43. Lamb Stops

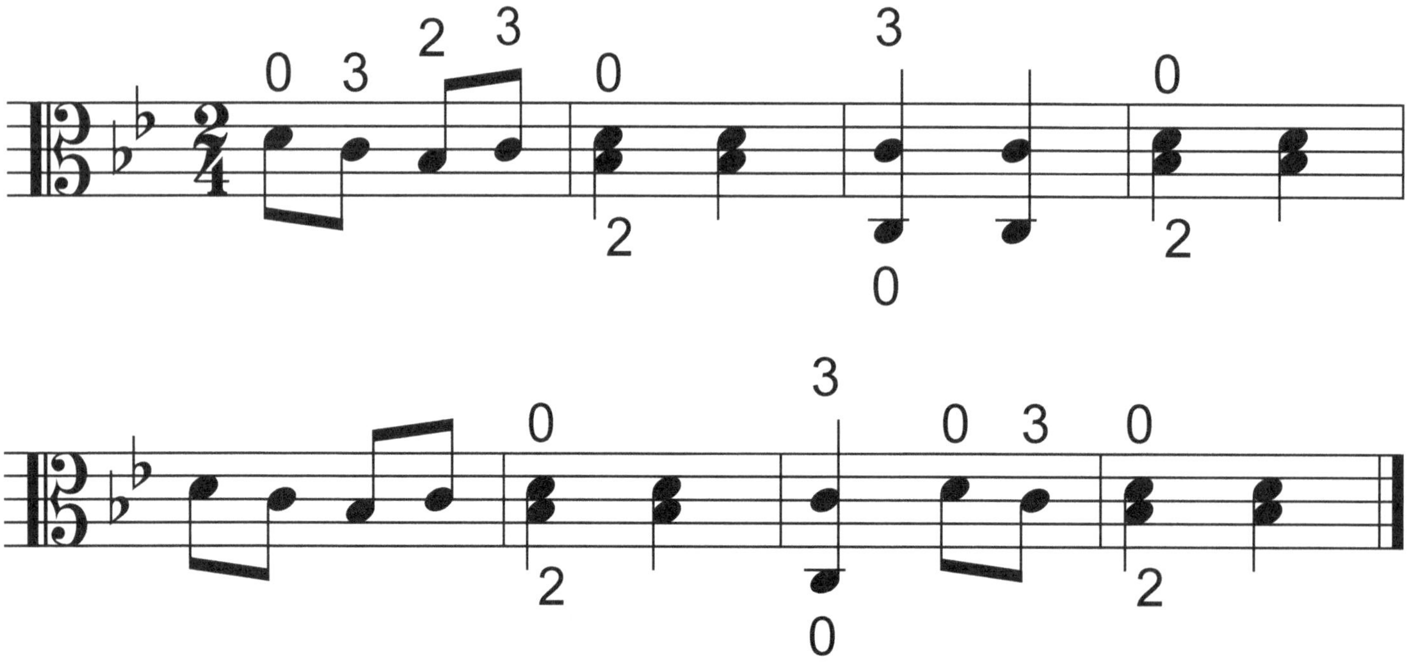

44. Mary Starts on Open G

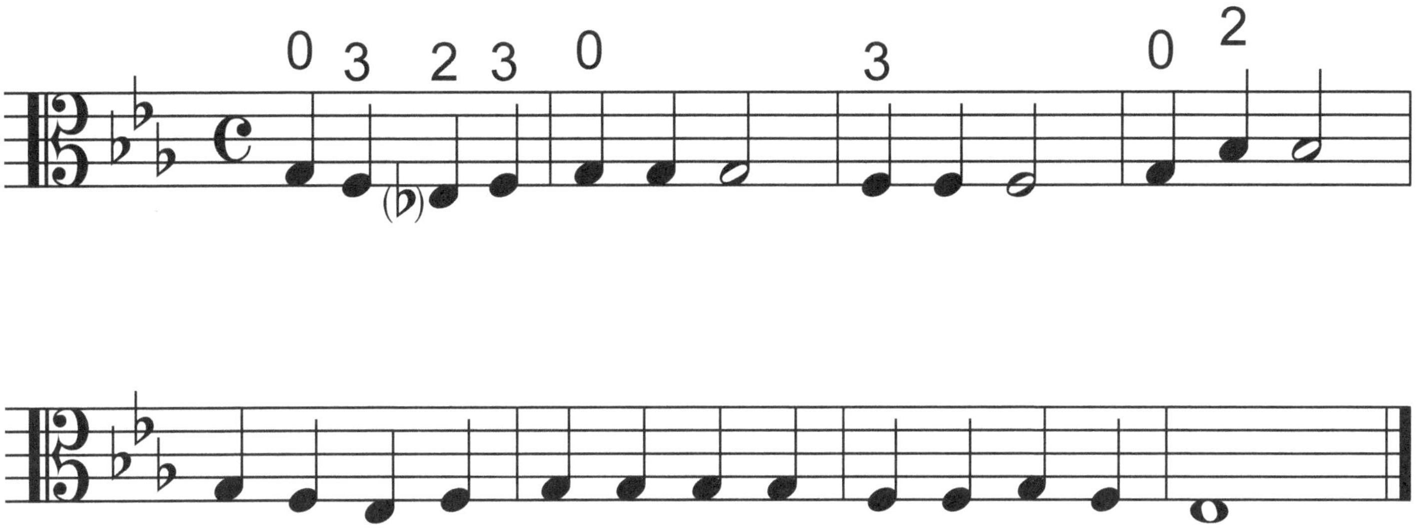

45. Lamb in 3/4

46. Mary Rests

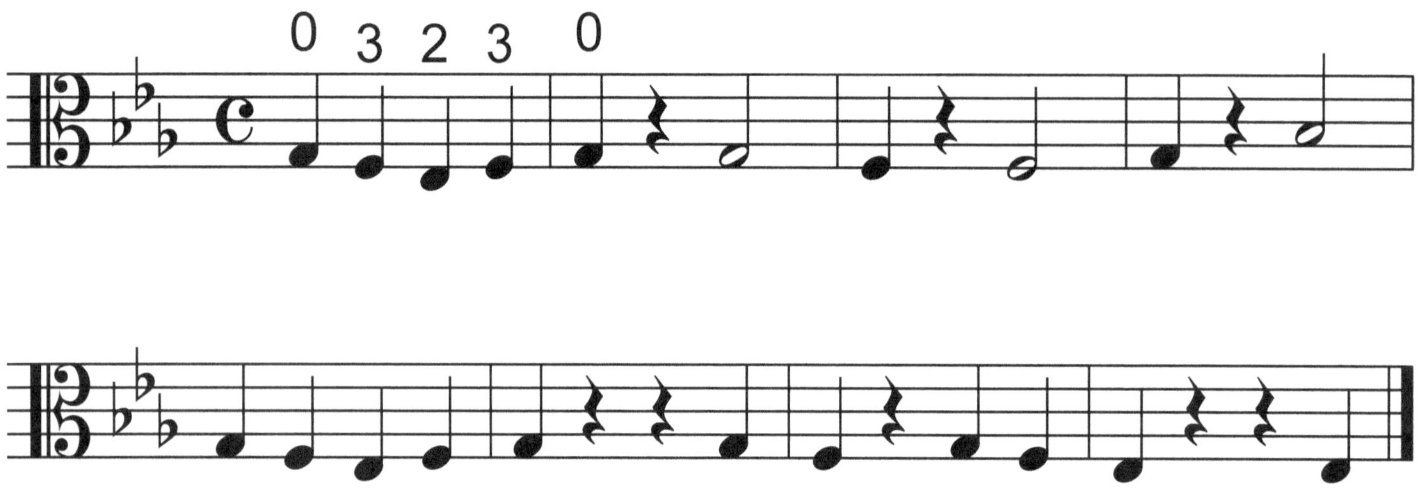

47. Lamb Octaves

48. Lamb Bowing

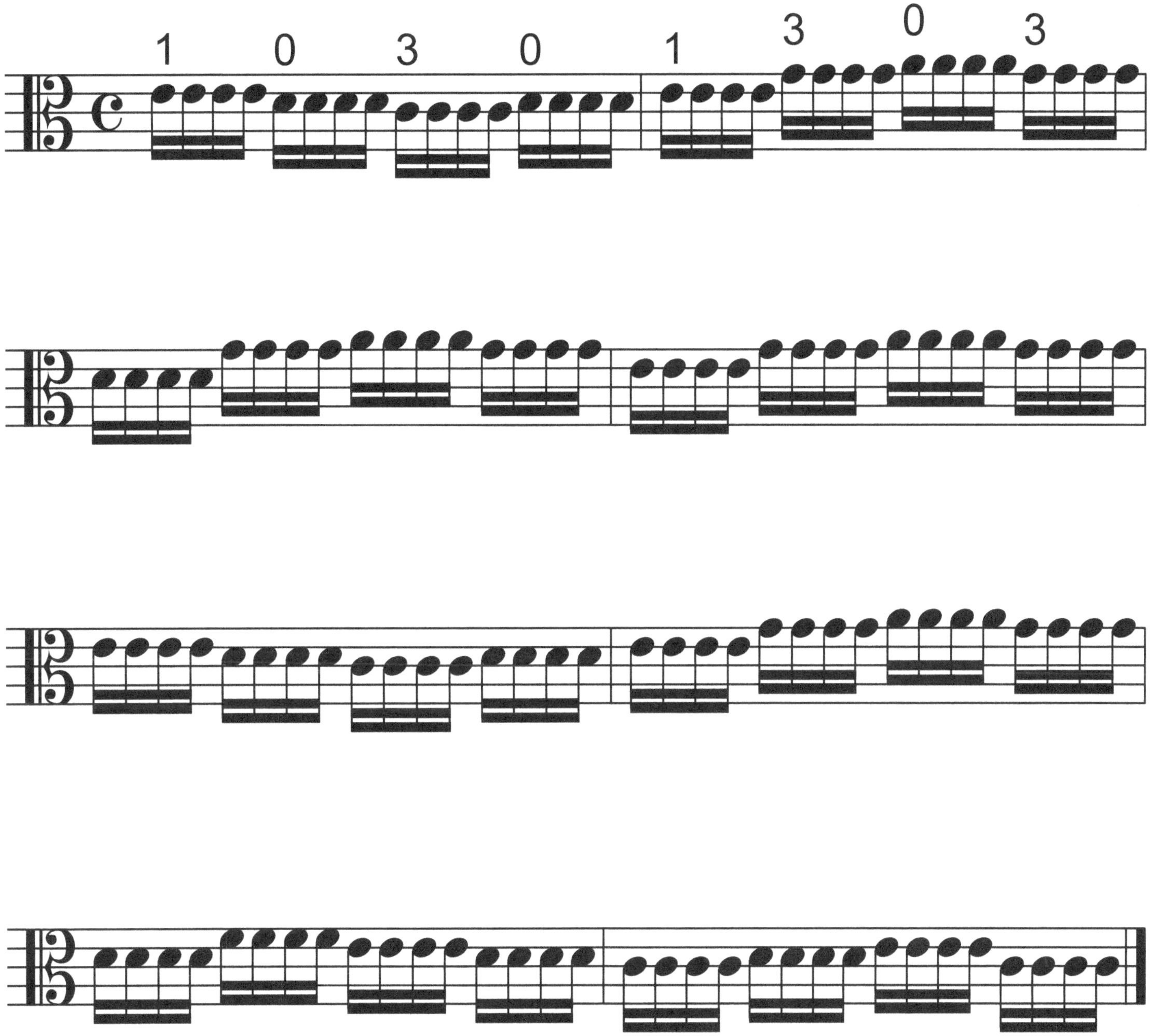

49. Mary's Fiddle Tune

50. The Lamb's Fiddle Tune

Beginning Fiddle Duets for Two Violas

Cripple Creek

Trad., arr. Myanna Harvey

www.ingramcontent.com/pod-product-compliance
Lightning Source LLC
Chambersburg PA
CBHW081130080526
44587CB00021B/3817
* 9 7 8 1 6 3 5 2 3 1 8 8 5 *